Is Anybody There?

Is Anybody There?

My Life as a Medium

Linda Dawkins

To order additional copies of this book, contact:
Xlibris
UK TFN: 0800 0148620 (Toll Free inside the UK)
UK Local: (02) 0369 56328 (+44 20 3695 6328 from outside the UK)
www.Xlibrispublishing.co.uk
Orders@Xlibrispublishing.co.uk
834304

Contents

I wanted to write a book to share my experiences of being a psychic. I still sometimes wonder why they chose me to read and help thousands and thousands of people all nationalities, all genders, all walks of life.

I was just little Linda Phillips whose mum had left and had a strange way about her because of it. How wrong they were.

This book takes you through my life with some of the psychic experiences I had along the way.

I'll tell you writing a book is an emotional journey only you can experience because it's part of your life, you cry where I've cried, your very tuned in

We are going to get very heavy into what happened to me, how I was to read thousands and thousands of people and the good it has done, also the fear and sadness it bought me.

Mediums have been around for a long time they were usually older kind ladies, now days they are younger and that's wonderful. When I came along and started reading in the early eighties. There were mediums in churches the odd one or two people reading through spirit. There was a strong belief there but no one to connect with until I came along. It's a wonderful gift, but it has taken its toll on me.

I was a fun-loving girl always laughing and having fun growing up, but even when I was young, they used to say I was listening or being nosey. I now realise it wasn't that, it was because I was psychic, and I was picking up on people's emotions. I could feel when anything was going on and I would cry if something was wrong, but because I was young, I didn't understand it, it was just who I was. It can be confusing for people going through it. I wanted to write this book to help people understand that they are not going mad, as I thought I was so many times. How and what happened to me I don't know and how I got through it and am here today is a wonder.

I would have loved two kids and a happy marriage, but life is not like that, but there are a lot of happy couples out there. I should know I've read them.

Television came into my life a few times early or late nineties, one of my readings went out on TV at 4am, I ask you. The show was with another medium, after that they asked me to go on another show, I said no, its Lucky I did as there was someone on that show that knocked every psychic medium that was there.

I've read many journalists and TV staff and they have all been lovely people but some people in the industry are not, they think they are more important and want to put others down, but there are those kinds of people in all walks of life. Take no notice.

If you have helped as many people as I have, then they can have a say about me. So, TV was out for me, a lot of TV makes money out of making people look fools, and as some of them people get older, they will realise that.

I'm in the real world, I've seen enough of it, people only recognise people who stay famous, they don't know me but do my voice. I never sat in a circle, there was no need for me, but it can enlighten people and teach you a bit about spirit, but sometimes you do get someone in a group who takes over it, like there is one with the power, but there is not, it is the energy of the group.

The only time I ever got scared of the energy was when I moved down here by the sea in November 2017. I'd gone to a place for a burger on the seafront with all the machines, I came home and went to sleep, I got up and put the light on and it went bang. The energy I've got combined with the machines, took the lights out.

The strengths I had as a little kid is double now, to do that when I moved here.

Sex can be very important in that you can get healing energy from sex if one of you has got the healing power, but because stupid people put labels on people we're scared to let ourselves go, if you fancy someone and no one is going to get hurt, go for it, enjoy being pampered and loved even if it is just for s short time, if you can find you soul mate for life you are lucky, lots of people have affairs, this keeps their marriages happy, no one knows, no one gets hurt.

My Life

My mother's parents were of Irish and Scottish decent and were born in Hackney, London. They moved to Southend in the 1940s to be safe from the bombs in the war. So, this is where we begin. My mother Eileen Strachan and her sister Jean were close and as the war was ending there were parties all over the place, people drinking, having fun and making love.

Eileen was going to see her fiancé Harry Phillips, she had first met him on Pier Hill on Southend seafront he was good looking, strong and a bit cocky. On her way to meet him she got side-tracked and went to one of these parties in 19 Pleasant Road. Harry lived at 59 Pleasant Road. She we only 17 years old a lovely nice girl (not wild like me at that age) she ended up having sex with a guy at the party and within that month she was pregnant, her dad wasn't happy at all. I was the result of a drunken night (no wonder I like a drink!) I believe we can have one-night stands, a baby comes along, that's how we get here a night of love and passion and we are here, and our destiny begins.

When she was 3 or 4 months pregnant, she married Harry Phillips. I was born on the 15th March 1950 in the early hours of the morning, so I was a Pisces ruled by Neptune. Pisces people are very tuned in and are the most psychic of all 12 signs of the zodiac. I am a strong believer in astrology, we would have more peace in the world if we used it.

Linda Dawkins

So, Mum had me, I felt loved and have never not. My mum, when she was pregnant, she wanted me, loved me and that's when love or hate starts in the womb. I was blessed.

The marriage didn't last 2 years Mum got pregnant again and Harry said neither of us were his, she had another daughter called Coral who after 16 years of age had a sad life and died at the age of 30.

The week she died I had a dream that the whole family got on a train, it was a lovely sunny day. We all got off the train except Coral. I asked my Nan where's Coral, she said she's had to go on Linda. I knew she was going to pass.

Dreams can tell us so much, we can reach our loved ones, or they can reach us. I used to go to mediums to see if she would come through, they said I had lost a sister. Many years after I was in the Westcliff Hotel, in Westcliff on Sea. She came and sat with me and said she was with all the animals and at peace, she smiled and faded back into the spirit world smiling. I feel privileged to have this gift.

Dreams can also tell us what can happen in the future lots of us have these. I dream in colour so do lots of people, we can also talk to people in our dreams and also there is astral travel, where we leave our bodies and visit somewhere or someone and then we go to that place we think we have been there, we have, in our out of body experience.

At one stage I went to Venice on a coach group holiday I'd done astral travel and knew this group, I knew everything about them we were so close for that five days and after I walked away it was like they were strangers again.

Sometimes astral travel can be our mind taking our body to someone in danger, can save life. Someone's mind can call on someone else's and warn them, we are all able to do this, we must never think bad in this as it is not right. Hate does no good Love does.

So now my Mum and Harry had split up, the hate my Nan had for him was terrible. My mum had to take us to her mum and dad in Southchurch Road, there were no benefits in those days just friends and family who can help you. My Mum was only 20 years old then, the flats we lived in have long gone now, but I'll always remember them.

Mum met another guy called Dennis and guess what, she got pregnant again, she told me many years later, she only made love to him once, but like I said that's how we get here. She had a son called Paul, who was adopted. I met him years and years later, he had a good life, so I was happy for him.

My Mum now had enough, two little girls under 5 and Paul was adopted, me being who I am kept going on "I saw that baby boy, now he's gone" She'd had enough. I admire all those mothers out there who stuck it out, but for women in those days if you didn't have a good man that was your lot.

We kept moving room to room at one stage we were in Seaforth Road, Southend. I was four and this is where I became aware of my gift. We lived upstairs and one day I was standing at the top of the stairs and saw myself go down the stairs without me, so my body was going down the stairs while my spirit was still at the top, before my body got to the bottom of the stairs I jumped into my body and felt 'I'm here' at the bottom of the stairs. That's the first psychic experience I can remember.

In the house that backed onto our back garden was an eight year old boy called Robert Dawkins, I was four, I met him again years later when I was 15, he was 18 and we ended up getting married.

Linda Dawkins

My mum had had enough and couldn't cope anymore so she took us to Harry Phillips's Mum. We didn't know her we'd only met her a couple of times. Mum just said her goodbyes and left us, we were standing there, me and Coral, who was only two, in the front room, my mum went to Islington and guess what, she got pregnant, had an affair with an Irish guy and had a daughter called Colleen, who I've never met.

The only link between me and my mother was when I was twelve. I had been put me to bed with stomach pain most of the night in the morning my Nan told me my mum had had a little girl. So, I went through her pain having this baby. This can happen, we can be miles away and feel pain from someone especially if it's a relative.

Sometimes when you get the feeling you must pop round and see someone they're sending vibes to us and a need, so always go by that if you feel to go and see someone, we're all psychic and can use part of the brain if we need to, a lot of people have this experience.

After this my Mum became a publican, had a daughter and settled for life, we never got close. I lost her a long time ago and that was that. I don't grieve for her, but I do for my sister Coral. I remember seeing a vision of her and all the animals she said she was with. I ran in the hospital to save her, she was nearly blind, couldn't hardly walk, she was put in an old people's ward, she was 30 years old. I cried and cried. As the years had gone by, we weren't close but when she was dying, I was there. She was a young woman, no one had the right to take her life, her energy or mine. After they put her in a ward, I went to see her, she was 29 years old.

Me and Coral our mum had left us all those years ago, I was strong she wasn't. I sat there and said to myself. I'm sorry Coral I should've have tried to get you back, she answered. I'm glad your here she went on to make up with her ex-husband, he did a few things that were good for her, her time wasn't then and whoever gave her that extra time. She's at peace now. She had lovely skin. I see her about 10 years old smiling at me, like in that dream she went on to a peaceful place, no illness or hate. The jealousy around her was bad.

⌒

So, after I was 4 years old me and Coral had a happy life with Nan and Grandad Phillips, we could have anything we wanted. My Nan had had a hard life, she was born in the workhouse, City Road, London. My Grandad Phillips was a paper man, my mums mum said when I was two I used to pass paper stalls my voice would change and I would shout out 'papers any papers' it's like I must have known I would be in that life. One memory I have of this time is my Grandad, he'd throw all his money on the floor, we'd be walking on it (no tax man in them days)

I used to go into trances at school the teacher had to shut the class up and try to get me out of it, they said I would just stare at something. I don't know what it was, but I know it was powerful and it gave me strength. I was only seven. Sometimes babies will look at something and laugh, they are seeing a loved one and this person or whatever will never hurt them. After that happened to me, I changed. I had my first puff of a cigarette and first drink (Babysham Pink Lady) at seven, I don't smoke now but still enjoy a drink.

In 1957 a lot of houses were empty, and my little gang went into them to play, I was always on and off saying there is a man there. I realise now I could see and smell spirit, they wasn't always good, these spirits were poor and there would be a funny smell and we'd all run out down to Southend beach and go swimming.

Linda Dawkins

Spirit do not haunt, take my tip, I speak to sprit and they tell me most things. There are two kinds of Spirit in properties or land, the ones who come back on and off to the property they lived their lives there and to feel how it was. Once a place is modernised they don't come anymore as it isn't that warm place they know. Like when I was at Trinity Road, when I went to view it a big man stood on the stairs smiling at me and a black cat sat there. I told the guy who owned it and he said that the big man built the house and died on the stairs and the black cat lived in the garden. I was there for 32 years helping people, now I have sold it and the lady is modernising it. They won't come back.

One of my clients bought a rural place with a barn and turned the barn into a playroom, her little girl kept seeing a little boy, so when she came to see me I saw a boy in buckled shoes old day dress, now her little girl was receptive to the little boy, he wouldn't have talked to her but just run around and she could see him, a lot of children up to seven or eight are very tuned in to spirit, he was linked with her, one day when she is a bit older he will go.

⚬⚬⚬

The excitement with this family was great to me at that time, at seven I could play on the street and I became streetwise, I waited outside pubs so I could help Grandad Phillips out, he was usually drunk but I had sold all his papers. we'd go on coach trips. My Nan would do us buttered bread and about ten hard boiled eggs, we ended up throwing them over the cliffs in Walton on the Naze. I think the birds had a good meal.

When I was seven, I remember telling my Nan I'm going to play with Billy'. One day she asked me where Billy was, I pointed and said there. She couldn't see him and assumed I had an imaginary friend and put it down to my Mum leaving.

Billy was a spirit boy, he was a scruffy little boy about 9 years old, I think he liked bread and jam but when I tried to give him it, it was still in my hand even though I could see him standing there looking at me. I didn't understand at the time that we are here and they are there.

The spirit world is peace, love and we're free. But the psychic world is different. I fought for 35 years to let people have freedom and believe in the spirit world, when I came along it was taboo but now after 35 years we can go to a healer, talk at a dinner table about visiting a psychic which is wonderful.

By eight or nine my little spirit friend Billy had disappeared, he went and found another little friend under seven or eight, they only stay with you for a certain time, unless they are related to you then they pop in on and off they look after you with love. No hate up there in the spirit world.

The summers in Southend in the 50's and 60's was great we could play out all day and evening and be safe there was our little gang with our dens, kids made dens in those days and took sandwiches, lemonade and sweets to them. There was Me, Coral, Valarie, Jean, David and Ernie and any child we became friendly with for the summer.

David had a 3 wheeler bike, I was mad on bikes so I got on it and went down the hill off pleasant road and I went over the top of it, I didn't really hurt myself it was a quick energy that took me over that bike, but many years later David died on a motorbike so looking back now I was picking that up but didn't realise or put the connection together. I wish I could have stopped it.

There was another boy I was close to, Gordon, One day we were playing and his mum said he could go to the beach I could do what I wanted so in excitement I ran out of his gate and a car was coming it stopped within a foot or two of me, my stomach went over I felt this from the driver his stomach went over and it connected with me. This experience and the one with David's bike were the start of me becoming aware that I could pick up on other people's feelings because I ran up the road to get my swimming costume without a care in the world.

My time to go up into the spirit world wasn't to be, this was just the start of a wonderful but very stressful gift I was going to be able to tell the past, present and future and pick up the spirit world.

I used to wait for my Grandad outside most pubs along the seafront, I had short hair, my cousins' jeans and I looked like a scruffy boy. I'd have loads of sweets, when I was waiting for my Grandad I would sometimes get into fights with boys in the area, the psychic energy would sometimes give me strength and I'd throw a punch and that would be that, now and again it would not be there and I would lose.

In the meantime my mum had come to Southend looking for a pub and wanted to see me, her mum told her to go to the Alex pub I'd be outside selling papers I was ten, well she went back to my Nan and cried how scruffy I looked like an orphan but I had half a crown a day to spend on sweets so I didn't care.

A while later I decided I wanted to look like a girl and have long hair, so it was to be the end of that era, I couldn't hang around outside pubs looking like a little girl.

Mum had long gone in my mind, many years later she told me her and some friends were going to come and take me on that day I was playing cowboys I had a cowboy hat on and a man in a big car stopped and said come with me but I said no I can't, my Nan, I can't leave her.

I was on my own journey to become the psychic I used to have terrible dreams and nightmares about a man after me and I'd put my fist through the window I'd sleep walk they put it down to I wasn't right in the head but what I was doing was taking the bad away from different people. They were all calm and collected and I was taking their bad energy away, which made me look like the bad one.

⌑

My first experience of someone dying I was ten, it was the man up the road, my Nan sent me to his daughter to ask if she needed any help. I went through, I saw him standing there looking at me, I screamed and ran out my Nan said don't be silly he's dead, he's gone I said no he was looking at me I couldn't sleep I was scared. Death wasn't talked about then.

Every summer from ten to twelve we went to my nan's sister Aunty Beal it was in Highbury, London. Her younger daughter Lesley was Coral's age, I was a year older. We had a lovely time, Lesley, Coral and Me, we were taken all over London in a little ford car, changing of the guards, Tower of London to my Nan in Southend they were upmarket Aunt Beal's husband Uncle Stan was a clever man, he liked you to use words and Lesley's sister Stella was older I got on with her and begged her to give me a little badge, black with white markings (ban the bomb) and she did.

Lesley was 11 years old and was going to boarding school so when I got back to Southend, I said to my Nan can I go to boarding school. She said you best get and help your f-ing grandad he's got to get home from the pub'. That bought me down to earth. so, he was drunk I said to him can I have a little party in a hall he said yes, it was Queens Road Southend, I had a brilliant imagination then and told my friends I was going to boarding school. I'm laughing now because it's funny, anyway the party went ahead and people went up to my Nan and Grandad and said we're all going to miss Linda, she'll be at boarding school. They looked like they normally do, not shocked and my Nan said we f-ing need boarding school money. But I would come home from Highbury and they'd talk about boarding school for years. I just picked it up and thought I was, I realised when my Nan f'd it wasn't going to happen, although they were rough and ready they were kind and generous people and gave money away like water, every year my grandad had a kids party for 360 poor kids who had nothing, Easter eggs for the kids in the street. I wasn't brought up with greed and selfishness, I was bought up to share and give, that's what I do.

You can't take money with you as you get older, my friend once said she didn't want to be the richest person in the cemetery. Money can't help health, love and happiness.

I was the last in the year off the juniors at potter's grange. I'd read there was a jewellery raid in Thorpe Bay I was only 11, we had a lucky dip at school, you had to take something and put it in a box and we all picked something out. Well don't forget my grandad was on the street, he knew thousands of people selling papers he knew the whole town and seafront so I said my Nan is there something I can take to the lucky dip? She came out with this necklace and other things. So, I took them into school. Miss Lee the teacher took it out of the bag 'oh how lovely" but I never saw anyone pull it out of the box. I said to my nan I didn't see anyone get that jewellery, a few day later the robbed jewellery was found outside my school, my Grandad and Miss Lee had known it was too hot to sell, a girl called Maureen found it and got the reward but it was me who was the one who got it back.

They always said I would pass the 11 plus and was very clever, but I was psychic and had this positive energy that everyone wanted part off, which was not good for me because it left me with their feelings, some good, some bad. I'd go to tea with a school friend and say something and the mother would say that's what her daughter says and wants to do, I didn't think anything of it but it has ruined my life even today people try to talk to me other than the reading they leave me with how they feel. I try to keep away from this situation sometimes my voice would change, and I would talk like them, their accent and as if I was them. I am aware of all this now but not then.

My teens were coming and that is where my nightmare as a person starts,

It was when I started going to senior school things went from bad to worse. The energy in Dowsett High School in Sweyne Avenue, Southend was so strong it was not a good energy from thousands and thousands of kids and adults one out of a 100 people had really nasty energy which spreads quickly, nasty energy can sometimes affect nice people as it takes hold fast where as good, nice calm energy takes time but sometimes nice people are more affected by it than the not so nice people. Lots of kids through generations have been brought up with hate, hate of the father's job, a neighbour 'he's got more than me' all types of hate at that time.

My Nan hated men, when I was twelve, she said if you get near a man, he'll split you in two and if I had a baby, I would have to hang on to an Iron bar for days. I was scared when a boy talked to me. I stood back. I made friends with the boy over the road he was nice, his name was Ronnie, he became a taxi driver and had a big family. He was a kind and nice guy.

Linda Dawkins

Hate is the worst emotion, and this is around all of us all the time, please walk away from people like this, they hate what you've got, who you are and don't like your strength. Religious people can be like this, if you are not one of them, they try to make you one of them, if someone comes to me and says I'm sceptical. I don't want to make them believe. I do my job to the best of my ability and that's it.

During this time my Nan was left money in a will. So, we went on holiday to Majorca Nan, Grandad, Coral and me. My Grandad knew someone over there a woman from Southend who had a bar out there, so he went to visit her and got himself stuck down the wine cellar. In the meantime, we were left in the middle of Spain, stranded not knowing how to get back to our hotel. I could see my Nan was scared, even though she was tough, we weren't on home ground and I could see the fear on my Nan's face. We saw a local taxi, and got in and I could feel he was a nice man, he couldn't speak English but I could sense he was ok, I told my Nan it was ok, I was only 12, we got back to the hotel safe and well, Nan never went abroad again, I did.

At senior school we started visiting haunted houses or they were known as haunted and we were out at night in the Dark, me Monica, Ada, Sharon, Tina. It was dark in those days, not so many streetlights, we would only have to hear a noise and we'd scream and run. Any empty house was haunted to us and lots of kids then. I was always interested in spirit and I used to try and talk to them and at times I would get a small response, but I was only halfway there to becoming the psychic I am today.

One of my school friends' parents were undertakers. I'd go there and we'd go out and trying to find haunted houses as we passed a thick velvet curtain, brown varnished coffin was there. I said is there anyone in there? She wasn't sure, I was fine as I got older. Thank heavens they have got more modern now. I saw my sister Coral in a coffin at 30 years old, it didn't even look like her a shell.

—— ——

In senior school I'd gone from a clever girl to a disruptive girl, also my friend Sharon whose aunt Louise Wilkins was a medium. I didn't know that at time. Sharon loved listening to her Aunt Lou and was interested in it. She told her she could be a medium, but like me scared to see them. I don't know what we thought they would do.

Her Aunt Lou was in London in the Blitz. She didn't want to go down into the shelter, if she had she would have been blown up, instead she came to Southend and became a very good medium who helped lots of people.

People are sometimes saved because they have to do some more of what they have got to do.

She'd gone to a place in Fairfax drive and helped a vicar, she did a lot of work at Hilldaville church in Westcliff. She had a red Indian guide and was a good healer.

During school some of the kids who weren't as clever were taking energy and strength from me and I was left with their vibes and as a result they got better at school, but I got worse. The same was happening to my friend Sharon who was in a different class. So, we were both in trouble, psychic energy is in every one of us, so if your child's cleverness goes, look into it, it could be being used, not vindictively, people don't normally realise they are using someone's energy.

I can see Aura's, they are different colours which show different energy.

Linda Dawkins

A white one is a sign there are high energy forms in the person's life, it means pure, honest and truth. Can show enlightenment, anything that's good and beautiful. It means there is balance and harmony in the person's life or can show that the person is undergoing some sort of cleansing or purifying.

A blue one good, it is a sign that the person is intuitive and love helping people and others often lean on them for support, they can be generous and giving souls are truthful and often open to new opportunities

Blue can also be protection. When I need to (and that's not a lot) I put a blue light around myself and I have never known it to go wrong for me.

Green or yellow someone might be going through an emotional time or not well, but it can be sorted out, blue is protection

Spirit can make lights flicker on and off, don't worry about this, it can happen they can turn a radio on as well it can be scary, but no harm is done to anyone, they use electric energy to do this. Electricity is a strong connection which goes with everything.

~——~

Sharon and I got in more trouble and our names Linda Phillips and Sharon Moore were always being called out as troublemakers.

I had another friend called Monica (she was also classed as a troublemaker) Monica's gift was healing especially with animals, she was always helping some animal needing care. I remember she took the hedgehog to bed once to take care of it, when I phoned to see if she could come out, her mum told me she couldn't, because her mum had found the hedgehog in the bed and there were fleas everywhere. 'She won't be coming out, she's got to clean the room'.

Another time her mum let her have a party for four of us while they were out, when her parents got back, there was 44 of us all over the house, it was all harmless fun.

Me and Sharon were picked on nearly every week. Then we both was packed off to different places, a policewoman was bought in to take me home and Sharon was taken away.

All I had done Was eat left handed and wouldn't change, I still do it today. I remember my friends with their hockey sticks following me and the policewoman as she was marching me like a soldier, I was crying because I didn't want to leave the school. I liked Art never did it anymore after that. Sharon had a more dramatic leaving, Sharon had lovely thick Auburn hair and liked her make-up, but it was banned.

Looking back, I can see the funny side of my school days, me and Sharon had gone from 11 plus to O plus.

When I got home with the policewoman, I could feel my Nan effing but not wanting to say out loud in front of the policewoman. She told her she didn't want her here and I would be going to live with a relative.

It seemed like no one was there to help me and Sharon, we were lost. I lost touch with Sharon at this time as we were sent to different places. I saw her once more and then not for many years We've met up again now and we remain good friends today.

The energy was so bad in the early sixties, governments were falling apart and that much negativity affects everyone's life. If the governments are falling apart the normal person is getting annoyed this would cause everyone moaning and that becomes negative energy. Bad stuff was happening, the Profumo affair, John F Kennedy, Strikes, aggression everywhere was dark. It happened again in 1979 when John Lennon was shot. I was going through psychic hell and these times through the bad energy marriages were breaking up, the 80s would bring a lot of heartache around normal everyday people.

I was sent to Harry Phillips house in Eastwood, I went to Eastwood school, there were lots of Romany kids there, I got friendly with Miriam, Theresa, Yasmin and Lynne. I was in the bottom grade now. A few years before my grandad had bought me a ticket for the Odeon in Southend to see the Beatles, it was great, I remember looking over two blond girls in the audience, when I got to Eastwood they were there. So, I was being shown I was going to meet them Marylyn and Eileen and become friends, which we did. In Eastwood, we used to go into school first thing to ger our mark and then went off strawberry picking, no more O plus for me.

Within two months I was back home in Pleasant Road with my Nan and Grandad, I couldn't get on at Harry Phillips house, he had three daughters and a son, and I struggled to fit into the routine of family life. In the meantime, Harry Phillips came to live with us with the kids. There were five of us in a bedroom, no bathroom or central heating. This next chapter of my life I am between 13 and 15, I'm not putting in the book it's not going to benefit anyone.

By the time I was15 I was shy, quite pretty with long dark hair. My personality had changed because, in those days you were expected to get a job at 15, but I kept getting nervous of interviews so was struggling to find a job. So, I was thrown out, they put what clothes I had then in a carrier bag and threw me out, my happy days were over, really since

1963, and on and off through my life. The happiest I am is now at 68 years old. I don't have to fight mentally anymore. There I was in the alley at the back off the house, now it would have been easy for me to have gone down a bad path at that point, but spirit were protecting me, I realise now it was because I was to become a psychic. I had met Bob Dawkins, the boy who lived at the bottom of our garden when I was four with my mum in Seaforth Avenue, he was eight. Now I'm 15 and he is 19, we met in the Cricketers dance hall, London Road. I was still at my Nans. It wouldn't be for long though.

I didn't want a boyfriend, but my best friend Tina liked his mate, they were always in petty trouble, long haired, tattoos, out of work. I was at Woolworths then, not my type at all and I'd been through a lot between thirteen and fourteen, I didn't want to know. Bob was a GI's baby, never did find his dad.

So, because me and Tina were close, I said I'd go out with him for that night, it ended up being nearly 30 years but he was going to protect me, I gave him excitement and he gave me security through our time. There were laughs, fun and drinks. I wanted kids, he didn't really, but he was to keep me safe until I was to become who I am today.

Within a month I lost my job and I was out on the street, his grandparents adopted him and bought him up, they were alright. His mum worked and so did his dad, a normal home, not like mine. He was into Ouija boards, he said a man used to visit his bedroom sometimes called Howard. We did Ouija boards a few times, I don't like them, they are mostly harmless but all you need is one person with funny energy and the glass will go all over the place and sometimes break but it was the 60s lots of people were doing it. My advice is don't.

Linda Dawkins

So, I'm homeless, jobless and only 15, his mum gave him money and bought him a van. One night he started sneaking me in his house, it went on for weeks, then I had a nightmare and they knew I was there, they were alright about it. When they were young, they eloped to Gretna Green to get married.

In the meantime, Harry Phillips was following me saying my Nan wanted me home, he came in the hairdressers and gave me a load of money. I didn't want to go back but at 15 years old I had no say.

1965 Southend seafront was buzzing, they would set up cafes, booths, no health and safety. There was an Indian lady reading palms. I believed even then, no one made me, I just did. It was about 50 pence in our money today, for a reading.

Bob had a van, he hadn't passed his test, I was still homeless and jobless, she gave me a look which sometimes people did as though they saw something in me. My dear she said, her English was good you will have a big white wedding, own your own home and travel the world. I believed her. Bob was waiting outside, when I told him he looked at me as though I was mad. Well within a week he passed his driving test. A few weeks later he got a job driving a small lorry for Byfords cement building firm. I got a job at wiring factory, because I was only 16 years old. I had to go home, I gave my Nan extra money now I was working, everyone was happy except me.

I told Bob we better get married soon or it was over, poor guy he still wanted to go the merchant navy. We had a big white wedding, found a little flat which we ended up buying in 1971, and I've travelled the world. Everything that Indian lady predicted all came true.

When I was 21, we bought a terraced house in Albert Road, near the seafront. There was definitely spirit in that house, the original owner has it as a boarding house, I could feel someone looking at me, I'd turn around and no one was there, under the stairs were receipts for the PDSA. I filled that house with dogs and cats and birds. Which kept the original owner an animal lover who was in spirit very happy, I'd see bits of her in a pinny one of those old fashioned floral ones, just a glimpse, there was also a strong smell of pipe smoke which belonged to the Navy captain. Our time in Albert Road was happy, we went to Spain every year, we'd go out pubbing. Remember Bob we were in bed and had a cheque for £8,000 we were going off to Spain to buy a bar. I was blond at this time, we were happy,

But happiness wasn't to last, over the 70s my personality shone, and I'd become very attractive, I was in my twenties. Things were starting to happen. One night after just another normal nice evening and me and Bob went to bed, we were sleeping and Bob told me something came up the stairs and tried to get him out of bed from next to me, he said he stood up and tried to push it away, I slept through it all. I didn't take a lot of notice at the time, but years later, I realised, it had been trying to get him out of bed because it was telling him we weren't to stay together much longer. Which we didn't, nothing was happening to me at the time. Bob said this energy was very strong.

I got a job in Southend Hospital with Tina, I loved it, I was only a domestic, but I was good with the patients, we all worked together then nurses and domestics, no one was better than anyone else. On a Friday we would finish early so a few of us always went out for a drink, pubs closed at 2.30 pm in those days, on this day we went to a hotel to continue drinking, I'd only had two lagers, when I blacked out.

Linda Dawkins

I was out for what could be a second or minute, when I came round, I felt scared. The fear I felt was terrible, I couldn't relax, I didn't go out on Fridays anymore and didn't want to go back to the hospital. I left just like that The last time I went to the hospital was to get my wages, that was when John Lennon had been shot, that energy at that time affected a lot of us, space up there is like a shooting star, it gets there in a short time. One of the girls I was with was a great friend, until that day, think it scared her too.

I was scared out of my life. I could see spirit everywhere, I used to say to people I was with, look at that man, that woman and they couldn't see them. I didn't want to go to places as I could feel the energy it was a hard time for me.

People saw me go from a happy go lucky girl, to someone who feared everything. I knew I had to shut up about what I was seeing, people were uncomfortable and didn't believe me, they probably thought I was going mad, I know I did. The nightmares were terrible I'd smash the windows without a scratch on me. I read so many books, they all said different things. I'd dreamed my Nan was having a nosebleed, after that I went to visit her and that was happening, how could I tell her to see a doctor, so I didn't say anything. Things like this were going on around me.

When you get this energy, it affects people differently it can be mild or strong, because I was being prepared to become a psychic it affected me in the most horrible way. I had to get through it. It showed me my whole life before me, I was only 29 years old. I spoke to spiritualists, protect yourself they said, no way could that happen. I had to get through it from day to day, I shook, I didn't want to go out but forced myself, this went on for a few years, I couldn't go in lifts, couldn't watch horror films. Once I went to visit someone and wanted to get out of there the energy was so strong

There were two books that helped me the most, one on tarot and one on the playing cards, so I got a set of both types of cards, they helped me. Never in a million years did I think I was going to become who I am today, so when I felt the fear I read or did the cards, it was like therapy to me, like someone would paint or draw.

Working with the cards helped me enough that I felt strong enough to get a little cleaning job in an old people's home, everyone there was nice to me.

The matron liked me to read her cards, the staff were laughing, they said tell her something's going to happen, and we should have the day off. I took all this seriously and said no.

All the jobs I have had, where I have stayed a while, we were all like a family, lots of the lovely people I worked with have gone into the spirit world. It makes me cry thinking of them. I was young to most of them, a lot of them where double my age. A lot of them gave me lots of affection and love and good advice. I didn't need my mum, I had these women who had mothered me, love and peace to you all Hilda, Doreen, June, Ann, Eve, Violet they are all part of who I am today. Not many men. Bob in the early days, Barry who I fell for, but he was gay, Ken a nice gentleman.

I tried a few spiritualist churches but in the 70s they weren't like they are today, I went in my high heels, there were a lot of older ladies looking and saying shhhh. So, I left and went up the pub.

I would walk into places like pubs and would see spirit people sitting or standing around, I learnt to just make out they weren't there. I had never known of another person going through what I was going through. They would have gone mental.

Linda Dawkins

Me and Bob were drifting apart, all the laughter had gone, after the experience that night it was as though he wasn't happy anymore. I was too wrapped up in what I was going through to notice.

I'd always wanted to go to America, so we booked a holiday. It was the best thing I'd do for me

The holiday was going to be in Florida. Disney World, Sea World. I'd be going through the fear a few years now, but the minute we landed in Florida the fear went, what it was couldn't get me in Florida, it was day here and night there, the fear had gone so I knew I wasn't going mad. I got back to myself, I didn't want to come back. One day, we were in a pub in Old Town Kissemee America. Where lots of Red Indian statues were and in the middle of the place was a spirit Red Indian Chief. I wasn't scared. They said he is coming to England when you get back, he is going to become your guide. I'd heard that mediums had guides. They tend to be spirits from people who lost their land Aborigines, Red Indians, Nuns all people that have suffered at the hands of greedy people I told Bob the Red Indian Chief is coming back to England with me, he's going to stay with us, he made a joke about him needing a ticket.

When the time came to leave America I was upset, I didn't want to leave but I knew I'd be back and I went many more times., I have lots of American clients and have read people in New York many times. My only regret is I didn't move out there. I wouldn't be in this pain now that I have picked up from the bad energy targeted at me by bad people. Not my clients, I've never read a bad person.

As soon as we got back to England, they were everywhere again, all around, at least now I knew I was sane and not mad. I told Bob I was going start reading and helping people. He looked like usual, he never commented.

My Nan told me about a lady who reads cards, her name was Tilly. Nan took me to see her. She was 70(ish) Catholic, very old fashioned, her son was in Parliament, she hated Maggie Thatcher because her and her son was labour. Maggie Thatcher helped me and Bob and many more buy our own property. I don't vote, they are all puppets. The trouble is with politicians is that they are in a bubble, taking benefits from the needy, and homelessness is so bad. The government has let this happen We all get up in the morning from a cosy clean bed, they are in a cardboard box it's too late for a lot of them to stop taking drugs or drinking. They are not treatable and for some of them it's the only escape they have. They were young once, with dreams, like when I was out at 15 years old. I could've been one of them.

Tilly just read cards there was no spirit being picked up as part of her readings. After I had visited her a few times I said I could do what she did. She bought a woman from the VAT office along for me to read, I didn't know much about it, but I did it as good as I am today. Tilly asked me how I did it, but I didn't know, it just came naturally to me.

Word got out and all the mediums around in that day turned up to see me, then people wanting readings It was a nightmare people were turning up from everywhere. I didn't charge at all at the time, people just put something in a box if they wanted. Someone reported me to the Tax Man and that's when I started charging just £5 for years and then onto £40. I am not greedy, this is my gift and I do this to help people and I have helped lots, and I know people appreciate the fact that I didn't charge the going rate. If I did some people wouldn't get the help they need, if I had I would be rich and be able to walk properly today.

Linda Dawkins

My health has been affected by people who didn't like what I do or want me out there. I wouldn't give in though. Some religious beliefs don't agree with what I do, I had a lot of Jehovah Witnesses living around me and I could feel their hate, I was called all sorts of names evil and witch. I'd go into shops and they'd say about Jesus on the cross, there are some nasty wicked people, I can't wait to hear what happens to them because something will. Karma These people did the most damage to me. I fought and fought the negativity and if I didn't have spirit with me, I would not be here today.

I started doing readings, some clients would make faces, some laughed. Then I'd start getting letters from customers telling me about things I had said happening. I've lots of them.

I started reading, I caught a couple of glimpses of my Red Indian Chief there were two different versions of him, one when he was on a white horse the other one was like a skeleton. I think they were showing me it was the same Indian in all his glory and how he looked dead but still moving about, a lot of people thought I was scatty and not all the ticket 'she's speaking to a red Indian'

The letters kept on coming, and I have still got them today. Crowds of people would be outside wanting to see me, and it was getting silly. I wanted to move. Finally, we found a lovely beamed house and moved in I thought it would be good, but Bob was never comfortable there. He wanted to get out of there with women he could dominate, so 1986 we moved into Trinity Road, I was 36 then, we had a coal fire it was lovely, I was so happy, the animals loved it. I was happy, the house was going to be for readings not for me and Bob. I know that now.

So, Trinity Road, Southchurch, Southend became the psychic house, people from everywhere came I was in books, magazines. I didn't really want it all but that's what happens, these days I would be on the internet, it's too much for me nowadays, I read, and I do what I can through the spirit world. I have done my job. There is belief out there, but there always was.

When Bob and me were breaking up his mum was alive, she said you can't break up, you got him on the right path, he would be in prison if it wasn't for you and I said he helped me too. When we divorced, he had no say over me anymore, he didn't get strength from my energy. He became a taxi driver. I have to give it to him, he was a good driver and loves animals. He met an older woman at a funeral, who knew the Dawkins family, he is still with her now, good luck to them. I don't shed tears for this chapter, I wish him well.

When I was sixteen, I loved him so much. Over the years so many people have tried to destroy me, a loving kind girl, that's what I was. It turned me off men for years. So, I had a few flings, straight women, good friends. This goes on today and it will always go on. We all need love and affection and I hope people don't judge me. I've never judged any client in my 33 years live and let live. Life's short.

I stayed in Trinity Road for 32 years, I started there knowing nothing about all this and ending up with so much knowledge about it. One of my early readings on Albert Road a girl who had bladder cancer, she said she was not going to have any treatment, she had a little girl, she asked me will she see her little girl grow up, I said yes or they said yes through me, many years later she came back to Trinity Road, her daughter was grown up and she still seemed alright. I thank whoever for giving me the strength to help her and her bravery to stick it out. There were lots of clients with situations like this. It doesn't matter if they believe or not can do something like this for you. They try anything, life is precious especially your children or animals they are just as important to some people.

They came lots of lovely people, two little girls waited for their mum while she had a reading, they were nine or ten, one turned to me and said I'm coming back when I'm older, and she did. Another one was a twelve year old boy from Scotland, his Mum said would you see him, he wasn't doing well at all. I said as long as you're alright about it. He came back in his twenties and it had happened, he had passed all his exams and was doing well all round. Fifteen is the age a proper reading is ok with me, as long as the parents are alright about it.

Bob stayed in the house, he had nowhere to go. I didn't want to be there with him, so I got a flat in Kensington Court. I had an office before on Kensington high street. They were surprised to find someone like me on Kensington High Street. They'd ask what do you think you're doing? I said reading. They weren't ready for someone like me then, they would be now.

The Arab royal family were clients and so I'd go to different places in London and read them. St John's Wood, Knightsbridge the readings at the time were £15. I only took what I charged. When I went to St Johns wood one day, they didn't realise I was a proper psychic, not just cards. When I started, they ran around putting every photo of whoever face down. I don't know what I had said to them, but they knew I was genuine. They took me to a princess, she was heavily pregnant, a couple of little girls were there. I said the baby was a boy, so they sent me to Paris. The last time I went was in Hyde park. They stopped the traffic and I went in the house with a few Arab ladies, after the reading the woman who called me to do the readings said they wanted to take me on the royal jet to the palace. I turned them down as I had two weeks of bookings, they asked me to cancel them, but I couldn't do that people needed me, so I stayed and continued to help people.

—◠◠—

So, I was living between London and Southend. In Kensington I used to go into a pub called the Goats Head. It was the early 90s the pub was opposite princess Diana's Kensington Palace. One Sunday the sun newspaper was all over the pub, we're all drinking, and the spirit world made me look over at the road towards Kensington palace, a black cab went up and I could see Princess Diana. I could have said something to all the newspaper people, but I didn't I kept quiet and gave her my respect. She had suffered a lot with stress from the press.

I kept seeing a little chimney sweep, he stood in the front room and he said (through my mind) he'd cleaned chimneys in the old days, he had to go to the top with a brush, he said his name was Samuel and had no home and lived with other boys and a man who was the sweep, he'd flit in and out over the years and one day he just disappeared.

I was always in London clubbing in the 70s and met lots of nice people, clubs weren't aggressive in those days, they were fun. I met a bunch of lovely people from Portugal, me and my friend missed the train back from London to Southend, so one of them put us up in Portland street, near Regent Street. She offered me a job I said I can't I've got a husband and a dog and I can't leave my dog. We kept in touch. Her name was Isabel Sousa

When the divorce was going through, I was really upset about the fact there was a prostitute's name on my divorce papers. I called Isabel and we met up again. When I told her, I was psychic she couldn't believe how much I had changed, I'd gone from a fun person to a different type of person, she had known me when I was in my early twenties. She came to the flat in Kensington, then I moved up to Bayswater. I loved living there, tourists, people having fun. I read quite a few stars, not that that was what I wanted, I was more nervous than them, but it doesn't matter we all need help sometimes. Bayswater was fun, the people were friendly. The Mews House was owned by a lady gardener who was Australian and into property. I loved it there but after 18 months I came back to Southend, because of my dogs and cats. I offered Isabel a job, looking after the animals and taking phone calls, she jumped at it, she was redundant and by the sea would be good for her, but we both missed London, her sister Rita came to stay they were good cooks, lots of garlic and olive oil, she had lovely parents, they welcomed me with open arms.

An American girl had arrived at my house for a reading, she was in an emotional state, she had come to London because she had seen a guy on the television and fell in love with him and followed him all over London, but he was gay so wasn't interested.

Americans are very easy to read, most are very open whereas a lot of English people are not. I didn't see this girl for ages, and I was concerned about her. Isabel is a proud catholic, so I asked her to go to church and ask where Barbie is, a few days later I had a dream she was living in a flat with a guy, so I knew she was alright.

She phoned a few years later and said she was living with a guy and seemed quite happy. The Church, Isobel and me had come together to find her. There have been a few situations like this, a top psychic who is in the spirit world now said to me that how I became who I am now shows that there must have been such a need out there for someone like me, and I was here to help thousands of people get through.

All through my life we had dogs and cats they go to the spirit world like us lots of them come through in the readings, Animals are very tuned in, an hour before you come home, they hang about the door wailing for you. I had a part border collie when I was eighteen, he'd been down my Nans because I'd work at the time. I lived with my Husband then, Whiskey the dog would always come home at six and I'd open the door and he'd come in. On this day I felt him at the door (by the way I am crying writing this) but he'd got run over I opened the door felt him come in, it was his spirit, his shell was on the road he stayed many years and lived through my other dogs and when they went to the spirit world he went with them and I see them all playing (I'm sobbing now so I've got to stop) I loved that dog, in fact all my dogs, cats and birds.

I stopped writing a while because I was upset. I went into the kitchen to put something in the microwave, I was just standing there when Whisky my dog appeared and gave that grin he used to, he stood next to me for a minute or two I stroked him I could not feel him but he looked at me showing me he was happy and then disappeared back to join all the other lovely dogs and cats I had. When we grieve, we can take years or it can be a short spell, something triggers it off after the pain some people go through the spirit world has told me this, I ask them, and I get answers. There is always someone up there who comes and takes them, sometimes people don't want to leave, they fight then let go and go into a peaceful place a lot of my clients have said their loved ones look for a long time at something, but they are seeing a loved one going to take them over into a peaceful pain free place they can connect back to their loved ones by dream state if you can see them like I saw Whisky because some of us can, they send a smell of something they wore or like when they said Dad died Tuesday but man invented time and days, when that wasn't there, there were no days or time. People have been so brainwashed and scared of the unknown, I was one of them but I was given this gift, it was planned the day I got here and I'm proud it's taken my life over, there have been some people mainly religious groups no one knows everything not me no one But I was put here to bring a belief in the peace and love of the spirit world nature, you can't stop the wind, rain and sun going on and they couldn't stop me. I wouldn't give in I'm not wasting my time knocking them they've got to face whatever's in the future as we get into my teens and twenties it gets serious the psychic energy and how it can become very valuable for the future and the world could become a better place for if lots of us. Essex is a very psychic place.

I had a Jehovah witnesses living nearby in Trinity Road, they didn't like what I did and would walk up and down the road 3 times a day, they followed me round the supermarket and restaurants. This negative energy around me went on for 11 years and it has made me ill. I am not a vindictive bitchy person but when you've been knocked on and off there is a time you have a chance to fight back. Go for it anyone who has suffered with nastiness you'll have your time to get back, if you don't want to good, but it depends how much you have suffered.

One client came to me around the time the singer Prince died, I said to him I've got Prince the singer here (he was a Jehovah) he is in a gold suit and giving you a card with tickets in, he said he saw prince twice and he was in a gold suit both times. So, I went up to the Jehovah's and told them Prince came through, I said I thought he'd come to the wrong house. They can't get near me now

Essex is a very old place, with a lot of history, some tragic, this can leave energy around which will not hurt you, but you may pick up on. There are some parts of Southend I can't go as the energy is so strong and, I feel terrible and I don't want to go near these places.

I do not believe people haunt, they come and go but there can be energy still hanging about.

One of my clients called in someone else to tell her who hangs about on her stairs, she paid a lot of money. She didn't get the answer she wanted so she called me, I talked to her on the phone and I could see he was a man from the past, it was a place he liked to stand. Please don't pay lots of money because they go back when they are ready, not when we want them to.

I remember one day, I was upstairs on the phone, I spoke to a man he was scared, he said there was a man is in his daughter's bedroom and she was scared. I picked up on the man and said the name is George and it turned out it was her grandad, just popping in. it put their minds at rest, no one haunts us, only peace and love comes from up there, never hate.

I have done lots of charity events, shows at the house and everything went to charity, I enjoy them because I can reach a lot of people at the same time, but they are very tiring. I did four shows in a year once.

I went to a dentist and he messed up and made my front tooth stick out. This made me self-conscious and I didn't want to do the shows, many years later I went to a different dentist and he did his best to fix it.

I remember one time I got on a train going to London, I sat near an older lady who was going to see her daughter. An RAF man came in from spirit and was next to her, I wanted to say your husbands sitting with you, but I couldn't. when I used to go abroad, I'd look at a little boy or girl and see them older, so I knew things were going to be alright

Once I read a twin and the reading happened for the twin, he came back and got his reading this can happen for people or a relative of theirs.

Linda Dawkins

I have helped with murders, finding people and sometimes saving people.

One day a young guy came to me and he said he'd got asthma, I said you weren't born with it, he said no, he used to see his dad, who had emphysema, three times a week and was taking some of it away from him and this was causing the young guy breathing problems, you can keep someone going and feeling better on psychic energy.

A young woman came to me, she'd lost her triplets, the message was she would have another two children. She had two baby boys so I was very happy for her. Losing children is terrible.

Ted Smith, a local was a regular with his rolls Royce, little did he know or I know I used to wait outside his club to get in on my night off that he would be coming to see me many years later, he always bought me flowers, he was part of the foresters pub on the seafront with his dad, Peggy and Teddy Feathers. They were a good lot. He died in Portugal God bless you. I can see him with that cheeky smile he had.

I'm very popular with the Americans and Australians and got lots of letters from them when they went home. My Julianna came in a blue rolls Royce with a bottle of wine.

My Road to Recovery

*I*ts December 31st, 2017, I am sitting in a lovely flat looking out of my window in Marks Court, five minutes from the sea on Southend sea front. But 32 years ago it was so different. I feel an overwhelming peace here, with my cat Brandy who also went through a lot.

My nightmare began many years before which will be in the book, chapters before.

When your different from being gay, to being overweight, a different colour or religion people get together and get nasty. I felt very alone, I was the witch, the fortune teller, had no gift at all and this was all because, for 32 years I have been helping people and not for money.

In my own town in Southend on Sea, Essex I could go in some restaurants and supermarkets and shops without hassle and lots I couldn't.

I went from a fun loving Essex girl to a scared woman, but I kept helping people regardless.

Today I am a respected genuine clairvoyant with a big following. My gift has helped thousands and I will still do my best while I am here.

When you're walking down the road go into different places and I can see people from the spirit world and I'm only young, I was not prepared for all this, the fear and the hate from people who didn't like what I could do I was scared but I would not give in and never will give in to simple minded people who live in glass houses, what they did to me was wicked but this is about my journey and my experience to where I am today. A whole lot of information for all off you to learn so there will be generations and generations who are not scared of love from the spirit world and to the clairvoyants of tomorrow which there will be quite a lot.

Its November 1986 I had been married to Bob for quite a while, since 1968, we wanted to move, more me than him. We found 145 Trinity Road, in Southend. I walked in, it was my dream after most of my life without a bathroom this was great. As I walked in, I saw a big man from the spirit world standing on the stairs and a lovely black cat. I told the man who owned the house. The man on the stairs was smiling at me, so he was telling me I was going to buy the house and the black cat was looking up at me. This form of spirit are greeting us and telling us good news. At another time I'd rented in London and spent a few years on and off, when I used to come home to Trinity Road, he'd be on the stairs smiling at me, he'd died on the stairs and my house was the priory and next door was the rectory he'd been connected with 145 and 147 a house and a bungalow I don't know how I would feel today he has moved up and on, the two places are different today and the owners can't see him like I could, they might feel but I doubt it. at that time the Rectory and the Priory were like when he knew it. over the years they have been modernised, nothing is forever, we must all understand that.

So here we are 1986 moving in, there was a fireplace, old beams, my dream home. So I thought my marriage was crumbling, he had done his job, he had looked after me and I was safe and a clairvoyant. I could knock him but this is not what this book is about and most of the time we needed each other but not sexually.

So, my journey to learn what I know should make people realise psychic energy is real and we all use it on a level of low or high energy.

There are and were a good lot of mediums out there. Alice Polly was one lovely lady genuinely cared about people and the spiritualist church has done a lot of good if she could.

A trance medium is taken over by someone from the spirit world and their face would change and you would see the face of the person that's with them, this would/can be very draining but I have seen this happen, it only lasts a few minutes then they go back up there.

Psychological stuff can be very dangerous to the mind. Someone coming into your home moving things is creepy, these people who try and upset people and their mind are not right in the head, please never go down that path because it catches up with you. A psychic will predict and pick up spirit they will never mess with your mind what you get for the future for the client is there, I'm just making them aware of it. On waking up early morning spirit usually visit. There are countless people who I have read that have seen and felt spirit around them. There is a great belief in it out there.

I was in London on and off for a few years. I used to read TV and film clients all lovely people, also some important politicians who I would never name or talk about, that goes with the job.

One day a lovely older lady came into my Kensington office, she said she wasn't the sort to visit someone like me but her friend had told her about me and she said why not, she was very petite and lady like. All of a sudden Princess Diana stood there smiling sweetly at her and holding out a card. I said I hope you believe this and she said she used to go to garden parties and charity dos and her and Diana would always give each other a card so she was pleased, it made her day. I was offered to meet Diana through Wendy Richard, I never took it up.

The last time I was in London I was in Madia Vale in the 90s I took the dogs and cats to a garden flat, read a lot of interesting people a lot from the theatre and TV. I was getting tired and the rents were big up there, so after 2 years. I came back to Southend, back to Trinity road. My friend had been made redundant so she said she would help me, a new generation was coming to me, my client's daughters and sons I get as many men as women people from abroad, America, Australia, Europe, they were coming from everywhere.

Isobel cooked, cleaned and looked after the dogs and cats. It was a happy time, her sister Rita used to come frequently from Germany, her husband worked as a pilot out there.

When I arrived back to the house in Southend the man on the stairs was standing there smiling, he was glad to see me, the house had been empty for two years, after quite a few years I had paid for the house

A soldier bought the plot and when the building society sent me the deeds he stood in the front room and gave me a salute I looked out of my window and a man was walking by, his dog who was in spirit was behind him. He used to walk where he took the dog for walks so the dog continued to go with him. As I was in the house 32 years people get jealous, they thought I was making a fortune

The first 3 years I never charged, people put in a pot from a £1 to £5 until someone reported me to the taxman. Then I started to charge £5 until it got to £40, but I have read and done thousands and thousands of people, for next to nothing. I never thought about the money only the person. After 32 years of doing it I was a broken person. Jehovah's following me about, some of the neighbours being horrible, I had had enough of bullies always need more than one person to bully.

Isabel had gone back to London then they had me on my own, it was a nightmare all I kept doing at that time was helping people. They would throw things in the garden, stand outside, six Jehovah's outside the house, I was trapped, they broke me but could not break my gift. I know what is going to happen to every one of them 'I say nothing' The next part of this book is about some of my clients experience of spirit and some from people I know there are thousands of them so I will pick out the ones that will interest you all.

Sometimes clocks will stop for different reasons, lights go on and I have experienced both. Nothing to be scared by this they sort out themselves. They can ring a doorbell also people jump and get scared I would have been the same but because I went through, what I did it does not scare me. Love never hurts and as they say there's no hate or money up there.

How I got through what I have I will never know 35 years is a long time of fear in the early days, helping people day in day out, lots of days clients crying and being happy because someone they've wanted has come through or their going to get pregnant when doctors have said they can't, there's hundreds of them now the grandchildren and great grandchildren are coming to me now.

I don't like to keep on about these bullies, but I don't want anyone to go through what I did. I am going to tell you one more thing and hope you understand how some of these people are wicked, it's not the church, it's some of the people who think they are God. God would not bully, prejudice or judge anyone. So here we go, it was lovely sunny September and there'd been a mugging in Trinity Road. The guy threw something in the bush, I saw it because I am psychic, the police came and whatever.

Linda Dawkins

I've got a bus pass so I thought I would get a bus up to the bank, so I go to the corner at the bus stop, I saw a Jehovah and thought oh no, anyway she said, did you see the mugging? Yes I said it goes on. What about God she says, so I said he can't be everywhere she didn't know what to say that was number 1, here comes number 2 I go into the bank, one of the staff comes running behind the counter puts her finger up in the air and says he's the boss, meaning God so I said he's my boss as well, she didn't know what to say. I thought there has got to be a third one. I went up the high street and have a coffee and who was holding a teacake and tea, was a woman who said can I sit at your table, she said where do you live, I said Southchurch she said you can go and have a coffee at the Christian centre. I thought I've had enough today. I am going to tell this one straight. I said also I am psychic that I'd read half of Essex, she said I was evil and not right all I'm doing is helping people they are not spiritual these people they're bad, the church should ban them. So I got on the phone to my friend telling her about this morning and gay marriages had not come about yet, so I said wait until the gay marriages they won't like that, so for the next few years I put up with it and did not give in to any of them all I can say some of you ladies get back to your fairy cakes and the silly men reading to a group of people so they feel important, get a life. There are lovely vicars, priests and church people who do a good job. So now I have said what I wanted we can get back to spirit and people's experiences.

These people telling these spirit experiences are real people, some are friends and a lot are clients who are friends after me helping them. They are all from different walks of life and if any of you wanted to talk them, I am sure they'd be very willing

Earlier in the book I told you when I was seven I had a little boy called Billie who was with me a lot no one could see him only me, lots of my clients have said to me their six or seven year olds talk to a spirit child, just say he pops in from heaven to see you, on the verge of being a teenager there can be a presence around, once they are properly a teenager they go, they might move things please don't fear they can protect you as well.

Nadia Cataldo

She walked through the door for a reading in the nineties a lovely lady with a great personality, well dressed, just a nice person. When I opened the door, you could never tell what a person had been through some of us have a way of hiding our pain, we all have strength. I am crying while I am writing this. I am feeling that pain she went through, her beautiful mum Tina had committed suicide in 1984, Tina's friend had found her Nadia had blamed herself for years, Spirit told me to tell her it was not her fault, she was sobbing all through the reading but said she was glad she came to see me and felt free to hang onto guilt that was not her fault was terrible she was still quite young. I didn't see her again for many years until 2018 she had found out she had breast cancer, she'd had two lovely children a girl and a boy spirit said she will get better and the cancer won't come back and that's what happened. We have remained friends a lot of my clients have become friends who else have I got after all these years of reading. I feel some of their pain now I am writing this book. Before I'd put a brick wall up so I could get through and help them. It was hard for me as I am a soft, kind generous person but I had to be strong anyway. Nadia and me kept in touch, she started a new life, moved back to Bedford where she first came from although she's part Italian and is with Tom who she knew before moving to Southend, she is very happy, one day we were talking on the phone and she said she was taking some flowers to her mum's grave her Dad is still alive and lives in Bedford. So, I'm on the phone with her and her mum appears in my front room in a blue dress with white spots dancing and twirling around while I'm talking to her. I tell Nadia and she says when she last saw her that's what she was wearing so I said she's smiling and happy and when you go over the cemetery, she is standing there with you God Bless Tina Nadia's mum.

Some people never experience any sort of spirit and some are desperate to. I can't answer this one because there is someone up there with everyone, some people come as a last resort, but they all say I am glad I came to see you Linda.

In the early nineties a guy called Jack walks in for a reading, what a lovely guy, kind, compassionate and fun. I saw him a few times over the years and we became dear friends, don't forget my friends or family have to accept me as I am because of the readings and taking energy from people and putting good predictions in. I am affected by them, it could last an hour or for days and would go on like them sometimes I'd say to my friends I need a break it wasn't their fault it was my job but I could clear this energy and then I'd wake up as me again a happy go lucky person, it rarely happens today. I've got very good people round me and they protect me here, but the Red Indians and spirit protect me from anything bad.

Over the years Jack started to get heat on his hands, he also loves to go to his church, one day we were having lunch and he asked me what his Red Indian guides name was. I had seen a Red Indian chief around him a lot, I said to leave it with me. I phoned him in the evening and told him they had said Red Arrow and he was a chief and was Sioux, he said he would look it up on the internet and Red Arrow was a Chief in the Sioux Tribe. I felt so happy to do this and so did he. Red Arrow works through him and he's a good healer, he is also a regular church goer and they both work well for him. I think church can be great for the right people like with what I do. I am the right psychic I know what I'm doing I never judge but when you're getting brainwashed from a certain person be careful we're all born free, sex and money are supposed to be on different levels, but these two make the world go round, without sex and money ask yourselves what you would do good sex gives you a great feeling but doesn't last, Money if your clever it can give and take you a long way but health is the one that's important. My Red Indian has arrived in the front room I've got two a bony one and a solid chief, one thinking about it they could be the same one, one when he is strong and the other one when he died he'd said it was in a massacre by the white man, now I am seeing a white man in a cowboy hat smoking funny sort of cigarette people have suffered all over the world because someone wants what they have got.

Now I am seeing five Red Indians in my front room all smiling at me this gift is wonderful they are happy they are in the book. Being psychic for me is there all the time, people are always trying to get one over on me, but its spirit there facing, and they don't win but have affected my health by trying to get at me and the psychic connection are totally different. I'm me and psychic is another link with me. So, by testing it they hurt me not the psychic connection.

Buildings will hold things from the past and someone will walk into a place and feel it, was that time not this time so don't worry a new group of people in an old building will bring nice energy and the past goes and a happy atmosphere could be good from then on. I used to be in the theatre club and go once a week I loved it most shows were in the Westend it was run by two lovely guys, educated about plays and films and they went that extra mile for all of us. Anyway, we went to see a play and a girl actor had the size of a ball in steel. I was in the front row, I heard her say she has dropped the ball and it wasn't in the act the ball came speeding over the stage the theatre went silent all you could hear was the ball rolling over the stage towards me. I put my hand out and it fell into my hand nobody knew how I did it, it was the psychic energy the steel ball felt from me.

Linda Dawkins

Once when I was selling the house. By mistake, I phoned the fax and got through, the guy panicked and said how did you do that. I said probably because I am psychic. I have to be careful and not be around lots of electricity it affects me, I get wary with light switches and plugs, don't worry not many people are on my level it goes with the psychic connection. Word got around about me and people started coming from all over the world. They would get a plane from New York, Spain, France when having holidays from Australia I would also be on their list for a visit then they would send letters over the years, pictures of their lovely children I could read from the photos, items any item, walk into a property feel the atmosphere see if anyone is around.

Over the years it has taken a lot out of me, the psychic side is something different, sometimes there would be a spirit loved one who belonged to the last client hanging around the house waiting for their loved one, dogs often do this. One day two different clients came at separate times, the first one after the reading went to the white horse pub, it's called the walnut now for a lunch and drink. The second client also went down there after the reading. They did not know each other, they got talking and became a couple. So, spirit bought them together. Lots of things happen like that.

There were lots of sad things as well as happy things, people crying losing babies, mothers feeling lost and fathers. I really don't know how I got through this 32 years but most people who came got help. If asked to do it again the answer would be no it took my life, my personality as I would be left with their sadness for a while and they would get uplifted by my psychic side, not me. We have all got someone or something that gives out an inner strength, when my niece Natasha and nephew Sean stayed with me, they for a short while went to porter's grange school, where I went. I walked passed my favourite teachers classroom, it was just as it was when I took them to school, the door of that classroom was open and Miss Wolff stood looking at me, she smiled and was dressed very modern like she used to, smiled at me and vanished. I was 30 years old at the time. I was seven when I was in Miss Wolff's class, no one else could've seen her only me. So, don't worry, she just popped down to say hello, she's not there every day, old buildings. There will always be spirit hanging around generations of people have been in these buildings, a few people have said to me in the corner of their office they could feel someone sitting there and watching them. Now 50 or 60 years ago an office worker worked there and because he spent most of his life in this office he would return on a regular basis so just pass that area and say good morning to him, he won't answer back it might even get him not coming back, people might laugh and that's good instead of being scared no one in the spirit world would hurt anyone. The hate is down here not up there.

My sister Tina she'd dreamed of finding a £1 note in the seventies a £1 note was a lot, she found the pound and we had a drink. Some people have reoccurring dreams of being trapped or can't get away. They are being told someone or something is not right for them and need to look at what's making them unhappy. Before some people come, they will put a picture of who they want to come through or ask spirit to let me pick up their loved one they usually come through for them.

I'd gone up to London to the spiritualist centre twice on different occasions. They were mediums, the first lady when I got into the room straight away said she did not tell the future. I said fine just tell me what comes anyway through the reading she looked terrible as I went to go, I stopped at the door and said a few things to her, she said I was wrong then stopped and said I was right. I used to read the psychic news she'd died. I saw that in her, it was terrible how she looked. I've only seen it once before, the other lady was a lovely kind and I gave her a message to get away from a man, she said she was not happy with a few months later she'd also died. Now I believe I was meant to help these two, but it wasn't to be. I never went there again. The spiritualist Association have a lovely lot of good mediums loyal to them and do their best for people. I was different I was chosen to do past present and future sometimes for 30 years and pick up the spirit world I don't morally judge anyone I don't lecture. I do my job to the best of my ability, like I said I never met a bad person, with the thousands and thousands of people I have read over the years. I read in New York on and off for a while, they love psychics and made me very welcome. Thank you, New York.

One day a young Indian girl visited me, she brought a bunch of roses, her mum had come to me in the eighties, she was in an office in Southend. I'd said to her, you're going to get married, live in Africa and have three children. I said to her daughter what happened to your mum, she said she got married. Had three children and lived in Africa and this daughter was told by her mum, if you want to see someone go to Linda, her mum lives in India now and is a healer as her daughter starts her life in London. She made it.

A beautiful lovely girl another Southend woman married with children lives in Florida, visits when she comes back she's doing healing and mediumship in America when she last came a Red Indian guide came through and said he was going back to America with her to work with her I could see him she will as time goes on. Every place in England someone has been to me. A couple of local girls came, and they went on to be famous on soaps and TV. I love reading TV and film people, they are not consumed by the ordinary way of life. We must all try and make the world a better place by doing a good turn for someone and not run people down.

Harry Potter has been good for kids as it opened a way kids can express themselves and not fear. One of my friends' little granddaughters said when she grows up, she wants to be a psychic so she can see her uncle Bob and her aunty again. I thought this was great coming from a seven year old. Three generations of people have had readings with me there now, their grandmother, mothers and young people.

What about the unexplained when a person is lost on a mountain or in the middle of nowhere someone comes up to them shows them the way out and then vanishes. Then you are somewhere, and you see a property when you wake up its gone. I've experienced this, me and Bob were in France we were put in a front room looking over rural fields. I woke up in the night looked over at the fields and saw a big white villa in the morning it was gone or not there. As I tell the future if I went back to that place a big white villa would be there. I was seeing what was to become. Just before I started to read, I was going through hell, seeing people, nightmares. I was scared really scared I'd gone from a fun loving girl to this person. I didn't want to be. I liked fun me and Bob went to a dear friend to me, she was living with a guy in Leigh. It was a warm September night, I had a scanty top and jeans on, when we got there we all decided to go up the pub, I said have you got a jumper I feel cold so I went in her bedroom and put the jumper on, it was freezing and I mean freezing it was a warm September early evening. Many years later she was found in the bedroom dead and had been there for a few days, now when we pass there is a coldness our spirit goes into a peaceful place and our body stays and gets cold, if I could have done anything for her I would have but she is at peace. I've seen her with that laugh that used to annoy me, she gave me a growing up call so when I say freezing, I mean freezing not cold. I have never felt that again and don't want to Death is not what we talk about, at times I nearly never put this in the book. Thanks Sharon, we are born on a day and we go into the spirit world on a day. Some people are scared some people are not as scared as I used to be but I have loved life and have fought because when I lost time I wasn't supposed to come back but I did and have done all this work to let everyone have a right to choose if they want to go to a healer, mediums, astrologer or psychic if they want to or go to church. I respect all this, people will knock this book but not one of them could go through what I have been through or do what I have done. I don't want a medal they chose me, and I've got through. Scatty Linda a liar, on drugs that's what they said when I was fifteen, shame on you people, sometimes I will watch television and see something happening in the future and will start phoning around, no one believes them. I phoned the mirror once about a plane going down. He was sitting in his little office, took no notice. Things are not given to people from these situations for nothing, gut feelings showing you what's going to happen no one realises the psychic is powerful and knows people should be listening. I'm upset about this at the moment because we are not in control, there is a higher being and it is powerful we are not in control remember that, doing right doesn't always make you happy I sound as though I am giving you all a lecture, I'm not because things catch up with us, it doesn't matter who it is. One of my first clients, remember I was still quite young I fell for him, he wasn't good looking and was gay, he was always around my first house in Albert Road, Southend, no way would I go to bed with him, a proper gay man, he went to Thailand. I had a dream he is coming back. I have changed its 30 years ago, we can feel love or emotion for a person for a short time then it's gone, why one of my lovely clients called Beth had visited me for years her little boy called Taylor, he loved football and I predicted he would go to west ham academy. He did when he was sixteen, Beth's daughter Chloe got into dance school as was predicted Beth used to wake up in bed and see a little girl in her bedroom, where Beth lives in Wickford Essex. It was very rural before her house was built, this little girl stood there in a white dress and cotton rags on her hair. I felt she had passed Beth's house on the way to church. Beth's house wasn't there at that time, she only visited twice I felt because the school had gone and she didn't recognise it as it is today, she got run over going to church at about 8 years old, that's what spirit told me. Her name was Emily up the road now to Beth's house is a very old church. These sorts of spirit visit a place where things happened, they have no time. These people who have had bad things happen sometimes I used to visit Southend High Street and could see people shopping a hundred years ago in long dresses. My darling dear friend Bob Caton had been coming to me for years, he's got 3 wonderful children. In his younger days he was a builder one day he visited me and spirit told him he was going to work in an office and buy a red sports car, he looked dumfounded because he only knew building work, a while after he got an office job and oh and drove a red sports car, he's had quite a few ups and downs in his life, he was very upset when he lost his lovely step-father and devastated when he lost his best friend Stuart King he is my neighbour so we are close, he came to my flat and he's sitting there and a black cat sat there looking at him, I said there is a black cat looking at you, he said it was Chilee the cat, he had a long time ago and never said goodbye to, he has healing ability his hands get very hot but with healing it doesn't always last as the hands get cooler the healing goes. I love looking at Nature the lovely green trees, the glittering sea and the blue sky we must look after our planet this is our planet this is our life, nature and the land.

My beautiful Irish girl Charlene came all the way from Ireland to London with her furniture, she is a designer, stylist and creator and was trying to make it in London, she arrived for a reading in September 2005

Taxi Drivers in Southend are the most lovely polite caring guys they have helped me go to place to place and lots of them have got messages and their wives have come to me over the years because of my early days of distrust with men they, without knowing it brought my trust back some of them are very tuned in and kind, funny my ex-husband was a taxi driver.

Linda Dawkins

I never got in his cab, one was Ian and his mother was one of my first clients, he was young 11 years or twelve and he said once my mum had a reading we would sit around for tea and listen to it. God bless his mum Anna Maria so many kids have been brought up with me, their children and grandchildren. We are in a free society and that should be. We are not free because of stupid people's beliefs. The amount of people that want to see spirit is unbelievable, sometimes I am just sitting here, and all my dogs, cats and birds arrive, it's so wonderful and they come right up and sit around me, looking up at me. We all must move on and that's where a lot of us have problems emotionally we get stuck, love this one, that one and they don't love us. Before I lost time it was easy to get into my mind once I past time no one could I was in control how I did all the readings for 34 years I'll never know. People used to send me letters and cards of how the readings went. I forgot about them and had put them in a box. I got them out and read every single one. They were sent from all over the world Australia, America, Canada, Thailand, Brazil, Malta, Spain, France everywhere one of the letters said my daughter came to you after she's decided to keep the baby, and another one lost her triplets and then came to me again and the spirit world said there are two more pregnancies and she said in the letter she had got two lovely little boys. So many of them, all lovely people. I'm crying now how I have helped all these thousands of people, I don't know all I can do is thank the spirit world for helping me a scruffy little kid hanging outside pubs waiting for my grandad to a wild Essex girl could do all this work, that was me and I'm proud of it, and to all those kids out there who don't have it easy work that's the way out, not drugs or drink. I could have done all of that, but I didn't and don't YOU. I have got to be honest I do like my wine, but I'm in control, my Red Indian's have helped me over the years 2 of them would stand by the bed and give me strength they smile at me and put their hands out to me.

When you see these horror movies, take no notice they are not real and hauntings on television are a load of rubbish, never be scared of spirit, they give love not hate, sometimes when teenagers are thirteen, fourteen they have lovely energy of becoming a grown up and can cause an energy which is not bad, it's a young good energy.

Well the house in Trinity Road was always busy, people coming, I always like to tape my readings it sometimes happens as the tapes says not always how we think one or two times over the years I would tape over the years, I would tape the reading and nothing would come out on the tape, then one of my tapes was found by the police in a bag of ladies underwear they phoned me up. The tapes have been thrown out of windows, stood on, because of jealous lovers or husbands I know so many peoples secrets I say nothing, I predict and do my job and that's it. When I come back and I will we don't all come back, it depends on what level we are on, here I want to live by the sea in California, happy married with two kids and no hardships that's all I ever wanted but I had to do this work. We don't always pick our destiny it is picked for us.

The two long term affairs with women, one in my late teen's early twenties and the other in my 40s they were beautiful lovely women and with both I had a lot of fun but nothing is forever, and I am glad they were in my life. Later years I have got my trust back in men through my taxi drivers and a certain guy who has helped me, my sweet lovely babes, as I am writing this a lady has arrived from the spirit world, it looks like Sharon my school friends aunt Lou, in old fashioned grey skirt and glasses, she's just sitting and smiling at me. What a lovely lady. Every now and again I'd arrive at a place of someone's house to help them just out of the blue they didn't ask me to come I was guided because I'm so well-known they'd let me in. I could help them for weeks or months then just go. One particular lady lost her sister, death is not what we like to talk about, but we all make this journey alone but were not alone someone with open arms takes us.

Doom and gloom and pain in the room, when we are set free, we meet all our loved ones, dogs, cats etc.

There were happy readings babies predicted, love and marriage, people getting better from illness, young people are more tuned in these days than ever.

Over the next 20 years the world will change, technology will be smaller, and a meter of technology will be installed in every household and business. There is danger of smaller islands disappearing. I hate saying this its survival of the fittest, a new sort of stainless steel will become connected with buildings not wood and plaster.

Space will become very popular, a new planet is found not far from earth. A television set is created with technology everything in one from this technology meter from the house to a big technology station, but all these people will forget about nature which is the worst thing they could do. Space planes coming, smart meters are long gone in 20 years. A train going from London to all over Europe, jump on, jump off, a sort of ticket system.

30 years not many churches left, a new spiritual way is seen but seen through technology, some of Scotland will never change. There will be new aeroplanes, different shape, but then we have the poor whose lives don't change. Hope they are not just put in Ghettos to get on with it.

The next 10 years from now. Some sort of Brexit deal, if you can call it that will bring the houses of parliament to change business centres on international business deals. It will be like gambling for the companies. So be prepared, get you companies international our gas and electricity put into foreign countries more produce coming from New Zealand, Russia makes its own EU with other countries, the national health a total disaster will fall and climb up again, but will be different, these people have got to bring patient care first and I've read a lot of medical staff and they feel helpless to what's happening. We need a system the rich pay for the poor or help at least.

To me I am a 50s baby, the 60s and 70s were great. I don't envy this technology generation, its empty how can you cuddle and make love to a computer and just say anything to a person you don't know. My house in Trinity Road had got tired for it 32 years is a lifetime the lady who bought it has changed it big time, some of them people were nasty down there.

When I left the man I saw on the stairs wasn't there to say goodbye he won't come back again, it's a new era. When you move your animals and your loved ones move with you, it's you they are with. The man on the stairs built Trinity Road but doesn't want to be there anymore. I'd kept the house as it was, the new lady hasn't.

5 years before I left one September day, I couldn't get out of bed. I thought 'my god, these neighbours aren't going to help me' My best friend was away. I had no phone upstairs, so I tried to walk, the pain was terrible, they broke me, and they know who they are, so I walked. My cat Brandy jumped she saw the pain I was in, I had two readings that day and done these two readings. They could not take away my gift that was there so they can all get stuffed. I am still in pain today, but I have got spirit with me and they will help me.

Giles came at 17 he is now forty nine. I told him he'd go into theatre and film he said that's not what he's going to do but he did he travels all over the world for media and has workshops in Soho where I use to go and read the up and coming actors what lovely people from all over the world. I was never treated right NO ONE CAN DO MY JOB and some of these idiots treated me like rubbish. I am sorry but their turns to come, my Indians are gathering because I am getting upset one does a little war dance. When you go to your psychic ask them or they tell you who looks after you, speak to them don't think your mad because you're not, they will listen and help you it can take a little bit of time but up there is someone for everyone even in our darkest times. I have been in a few in my life some of my clients would come in their cars and I knew they were coming in to have a reading and at times a person from the spirit world, usually a relative would be sitting with them I'd tell them I could see them they cant. The police will use good psychics as time goes on, they sometimes do today. Some people want proof all the time it's the it's the unknown. We're not meant to know it all, no one does.

Tallulah, one of my clients lovely daughter when her mums partner died he come through with a cowboy hat and guitar Tallulah saw flashes of light and orbs around the room when he died, because of 32 years of reading in Trinity road, Southend spirit was always around dogs, cats, loved ones waiting for their relative to visit sometimes they would hang about for days until they came for a reading. Bob my dearest friend who lost his best friend Stuart, it was Bob's birthday and we passed the pub that his friend Stuart drank in, he was Scottish and outside the pub were blue and white balloons and spirit said tell Bob the balloons are for him to say Happy Birthday the Scottish flag is blue and white from Stuart. Bob was happy, he loved his mate Stuart. Day in and out I was doing readings, I'd had enough, they would bring in depression and I would get down feeling from some of the clients, their sadness and pain, but because my personality is bubbly I'd get out of it quickly. One of my friends I told them to take me around all the places he'd lived in and see what I felt. The first one was in Shoeburyness in Essex I said one of his children was conceived here and he said yes, his second child a son. Over the weeks he took me to a few properties one was when he was two years old as we came to it I felt scared he said I was right he used to have nightmares because of a picture on the wall and was scared now this happened 58 years ago the gift I've got is really marvellous. The next one I just saw him swinging on a gate about 8 years old but he did get on the roof in the church in Westcliff and rang the church bell on top of the roof someone called the police and fire brigade, someone said there was a child up on the roof by the time they got up there he'd got down and run off, he was a little so and so. One of the flats a man had hung himself that he lived in, he took some photos and the man's face came out in the photo. The chemist who developed the photos recognised the man because he used to go into the chemist, this form of spirit is rare but his death was so dramatic his form of his own self stayed in the flat his spirit went into a peaceful place and he got his peace.

I was being worn down in Trinity Road after 32 years of readings there. I needed a new start.

My taxi drivers like I said have been marvellous, one lady Candice used to pick me up at regular times, she's got two lovely daughters but had come away from their dad. I used to say to her every time I got in the cab. Candice you're going to meet a man who's good and have a little boy. Well once I got in the cab, I said you've met somebody haven't you she said yes and had become happy and has had a little boy who is beautiful and clever. I was becoming ill in Trinity road, like I said I was a broken person I'd had it, 35 years of helping people had took its toll. I'd started young and vibrant now I was getting on and not well. Generations had been through the door for readings. I'm proud I never made money the important thing I thought of was the person not the money, people should be learning from me not knocking and hounding me, all over the place could only go to a few restaurants in Southend who did not judge me or make silly religious comments, a Chinese called Pearl Dragon on Southend seafront. If you want an excellent Chinese Jimmy and Linda will look after you and the staff, the Salsa a Portuguese restaurant. My best friend Isabel born in Portugal had to go in there and ask if I go in there alone would they look after me and they always have, and an Italian restaurant called Ask, lovely people, kind, treated me like a person, this is what I had to put up with day in and day out because I was psychic and born and bred in Southend this shouldn't have happened. I would not give into these people but my body was affected not the psychic side of me, it will be there till the day I die animals have strong healing ability and will lick where the problem is, we should learn from them as well, we're all here for a reason, whether it's to have children or save people's lives, but we get bogged done by pettiness. Yoga and meditation are very popular these days also Buddhism and lots of people have stopped eating meat, animals should not be killed to give us pleasure, if you are starving that's a different situation.

I am really coming to an end living in my house in Trinity Road, the last year was terrible there I didn't feel the same about that house like I did in 1986 I loved it there but deep down I knew I would not stay forever, the man on the stairs when I moved in has long gone, the house is now modernised to a high standard and the lady loves it there like I did once. Nothing is forever, I've started crying. I've just seen all my dogs and cats here and my birds and the foxes I've helped all standing around me in this new apartment I'm in. it's a wonderful gift and that's what it is a gift from god and nature and all you psychics, young and mature be proud to be one, take no rubbish from nasty people. To all my clients Thank you for letting me into your lives, I'm grateful and I mean that from the bottom of my heart, a new beginning is on the horizon. I've put the house up for sale its 2017. What a nightmare that was, the first agent I chose sold it for me EPC in Chalkwell, some of the others just, I'm not saying what I would like to say, I've moved on.

I looked at an apartment and that's the one I wanted and that's the one I got. Coming out of Trinity Road was the best thing I'd done. I got an apartment 5 minutes from the sea, 2 bedrooms, the complex was built in 1986 and a famous footballer and his wife owned it then it went to one of his sons who I bought it from. Like I said a few times I was broken, I didn't want to do readings anymore I didn't know what I wanted, after a few weeks off I felt good, the caretaker Martin and his wife Ann were brilliant and very helpful and up to when they retired came saw I was alright, a lovely caring couple.

I've loved many people remember there are different kinds of love. Loving someone is good and no jealousy because people are going to do what they are going to do, if we don't marry the man we love at one time we're not meant to and there will be someone else for us and when we look back at the person we were going to marry all them years ago we know it was not right every now and again, someone does go back and it works well, the time is right but it's not everyone it works for, people get unhappy and look back at the past but they're two different people now, and have nothing in common.

America has big changes the next 5 or 6 years, a woman will be elected as president a very kind, honest woman for the people. England changes its political situation in 5 years' time, new parties form and politics become different, about time, a lot of them talk in figures and don't know the real world and people. The people that run this country know nothing, a higher force and I've been part, is starting to get through which means change in old ways and tradition people want answers and that's what I give them.

No one can do that and maybe will never again. That wild Essex girl with my sisters Tina, Sue and Val we had many laughs and a lot of sadness but have come through it and have become the good people we always were. Hate and Jealousy can do so much damage and the damage certain people done to me, but that's gone. I am respected because of who I am and what I do and so I should be, now I am in this apartment I'm this 15 year old girl who had all the good taken from me and now I'm me again, what a journey it's been.

My psychic power is much stronger than ever and there's a new generation that are strong believers, so Essex is very tuned in, lots off spirit around most houses someone visits from the spirit world. Love stays forever, please to all of you who reads this book don't hate it's a waste and only hurts the person who is hating in the end. We all make mistakes in life I've made many. When I worked in the hospital 1978 when people were dying they'd look and talk about someone, people used to say, oh Mum's going funny, today it is accepted and understood, I have seen a lot of spirit in my time everywhere I go they're around, mostly with a loved one, it's a pity we can't all see them but you have to go up and connect in the spirit world and that's what I did, I was working at the hospital 1978 and me and a best friend at that time Christine went to the pub at lunchtime and went to a hotel along the seafront. I went out for the count, I only had two lagers, we picked up this idiot who bought us champagne, I had one glass of it. That day changed both of our lives Christine died years later, I was so scared I was seeing spirit people all over the place remember its 1978/1979 no one had come along like me no one would have got through what I've been through. It's taken me 40 years to get me back as me, I am now 68 years old day in day out helping people you can thank that idiot who gave me the champagne, by the way he was a member of parliament some of them think they are higher than us well he wasn't higher than me and will never be he can get stuffed, sorry everyone but this has brought up memories from then that started it all off, he called himself Mr Cox a false name like he was, but I thank every one of you for coming to me I care about you all and hope your readings have gone well.

This journey has been long and hard for me because I was a fun girl always laughing, now I'm getting old and when I get up there I will greet everyone one of you who have been to me we'll have party after party and If I can help you from up in the spirit world I will. Nothings forever do good and good in the end will come to you. I will never write a book again it's too heart-breaking nowadays I live in Mark's court 5 mins from the sea, my dear friends look after me

Sharon Rutherford, Isabel Sousa, Rita R, Jack, Naida, Charlene, Sam Rutherford, Gina Jones, My cat Brandy, Bob's dog Tyson.

And to all the people who done me good, Doreen Padley, Brenda, June Gillette, Brenda, Miss Ann Smith, Rosie Lord, Tina Bull, Rosie Lord, Monica Wakeman, Mrs Wills, Barbara Rayleigh, Muriam Buckley, Lynne Cole, Mrs Brand, Mrs Kaulman, Bob Dawkins.

Spiritual Skills and Tools

Everyone has got some psychic ability like knowing someone's going to phone, someone is ill or thinking you're going to bump into someone. This is normal.

Telepathy is another strong thing and the wrong person can get into someone's mind. I've had it myself, when I was younger, it's dangerous when it is someone who wants control. It can change your personality for a time, if you feel anything like that around you step back from who you think it is.

When scientists put people in two different rooms with an envelope, they are stupid he's got a name in that envelope what is it? Were stupid what help is that doing for anyone if two people and you could get a cure for this or that. That's a breakthrough. Don't let people who think they know more than us bluff you, our minds are strong, stick together for good, don't listen to nutcases spreading bad.

I can hold items and from them can pick up things about the people who owned them. This is called Psychometry, you can hold a letter, a piece of jewellery or any item and you can feel the person who owned it. I don't have many things from charity shops for this reason, I give to them instead.

Tarot cards are ancient cards and were banned because of the honesty.

There are five cards that I have never seen out together and I hope I don't.

The Tower – which means a great big change around can be bad for a while

The Devil – Saying we're chained to something or someone (I don't believe in the word Devil and never will)

The Moon – means deceit, lies, someone you can't trust.

Death – does not always mean a death

I'd say it rare, for these to come out together, I've never seen it

My friend Gina got a set of Tarot cards and did a reading for her Nan, three of those cards came out, The Tower, the Devil and Death. She didn't think much of it at the time as she was new to it, but her Nan died later that year. Both her and her mum remembered the reading she had done at the beginning of the year.

The tarot cards did not make this happen, it was going to happen, she said to me it was strange, there was just no future in the reading at all.

The playing cards are not so heavy, unless you get all spades, also never seen them all out.

When you next take flowers to your mum or whoever remember they are there standing looking at, is my boy alright he's kneeling down crying talk to him or her when you get there be a sign or a dream unless your against this which is sad. We all want our loved ones to be happy and loved in life and in the spirit world.

Linda Dawkins

There is a lot about crystals, feathers and angels. I have experienced feathers because they are light spirit can put them anywhere where there has been sadness. So, you find a feather it is to do with a loved one. Birds are messengers of Angels.

I wasn't sure, then a lady came for a reading and two little angels one in a purple little dress and one in red, they were jumping all over the table. I said do you believe in Angels because these two are here, yes, she said. When she went, they jumped on her shoulder and went out with her, what could I say

Crystals and stones have been around for a long time and some of them come with healing.

Healers – we've all got the ability to heal, it goes back centuries, when I do a reading, I get into part of the brain the person also feels a good feeling for a little while. I don't if I get in a taxi and someone has been crying, I will cry.

Healing, you should feel heat on the parts of your body especially your hands, it has to be done regularly to get a response. A taxi driver picked me up. I get a lot of cabs, I have never met a bad one like I have never had a bad client, so that says a lot.

One day this lovely taxi driver was telling me about his back, he was crawling about and said he'd try anything to be out of pain he went to a faith healer on Canvey Island and the healing lasted about 6 months then his back pain started again, he ended up having an operation. Healing I have found has to be done regularly to work. Me and Bob went over and had a drink in Colchester, Bob had terrible hay fever, the publican said he could cure it, he went to a pond and got a jar of pond water and told him to drink it, he never got hay fever again, there are remedies that work, that go back to the old days.

There are some good healers out there so there is nothing to lose if you're in pain

Testimonials

Tomorrow, yesterday, and today I will miss you, and still
be missing you for ever in my heart love Isobel xx

Linda was one of my dearest friends. Loyal, fun, caring and extremely gifted. She
had a wonderful personality and when we used to meet up or chat on the phone
there was always lots of laughter. Linda was just an amazing human being who
was kind and generous - a great friend, A true Star. She is greatly missed.

Jack

Linda Dawkins my dear friend who I meet at school when we were 11
wonderful memories, I have of her, she was Linda Phillips then, as the
years went by she became a Truly gifted unique Lady and my friend,
she helped so many people with her gift and was a true giver.
I want to thank you for the positive way you helped me over the year's I
will miss you so much and will never forget you and I won't be alone Linda
Phillips & Sharon Moore please stand up. She will smile when she sees
this lots love bet you are making a lot of people laugh where you are.

Sharon

My sister was funny, selfless and one of the kindest people I know, if anybody needed help or anything she would help. Like taking me out for a meal when times were hard. Linda gave me her first set of tarot card from the USA she couldn't read then as didn't feel right. she said they would suit me better as I would become a medium, and when you do, you will get fat sitting down reading, her sense of humour was priceless I miss you so much but feel you near love you Linda

Tina

Oh how much I miss Linda. I have her voice recorded on my phone and every time I hear her it makes me smile. My path to find Linda just happened as it usually does in these circumstances and over the years - her messages were always spot on. I am so fortunate to have spent her last Christmas Day with her and my Mum Sharon. I have a message she left for me early that Christmas morning that I play when I need strength and support. I know she is with us always and very busy talking to all the connections she made down here that now reside in the next plane including my Great Aunt Lou. She taught me so much and I hope to keep evolving with my own spiritual quest as she predicted. Love you with all my soul Linda. Till we meet again x

Sam

Sisters — the days leading up to Lin's death, Lin saw our Nan, our sister Coral and her little dog Sophie which were all in the spirit world. Lin said to us, what have I done with my life, we told her that she had helped thousands and thousands of people. We told her we loved her, the last words Lin said was I love you. Sadley Lin passed on 14ᵗʰ March 2019, God bless you Lin

Sue and Val

I feel extremely lucky to have Linda as a friend, and know she is still with us. She was a pure, kind and loving person, one of a kind. A very special lady and the most amazing medium I have ever met. I am grateful to have worked with Linda to create this book and proud to see her final wish realised.

Gina

Printed in Great Britain
by Amazon